# The BIG Question MARK

UZAIR M. GHOLE

outskirtspress
DENVER, COLORADO

Outskirts Press, Inc.
http://www.outskirtspress.com

ISBN: 978-1-4787-4444-3



PRINTED IN THE UNITED STATES OF AMERICA

*Special Thanks to:*

*Mr. Zafarulah Khan, My Nephew in Laurel, Maryland*

*Mr. Fazle Khan, My Nephew in Booklyn, New York*

*Mr. Hamza Abdul Malik Long Island, New York*

*Mr. Robin Albert Peter. Pakistan Born Christian (Now in USA.)*

*who gave me inspiration to think about what I have been following since my childhood and what is supposed to be followed, leading me to the study of comparative world religions and the truths and mysteries and myths of the concept of God and its religion.*

# Index:

# Introduction:

I am Uzair M. Ghole, a common man like the billions of people of the world, which always makes me realize how small I am or how big I am. I was raised in India, in a middle-class family with two siblings and my parents. We lived in a village called Kemburly, situated near the mountains and rivers a few miles away from the city of Maharashta, called Mahad (India).

Father decided to move away to a developed place called Navi-Mumbai (Panvel), which is approximately 100 miles away from Kemburly, in search of advancement in life progress and prosperity.

Let me talk about me even before my existence. The reason I am talking about this is to throw light on further topics of life reality and the question of the existence of God.

This is not a big concept or topic that has to be difficult for every single human being to understand the big question, like DOES GOD EXIST? It has to be understood by each one of us.

It's simple, as well as complicated; it can be understandable through the signs and signals which we are seeing every single day, but still we are in search of the same answer to that question.

Many scientists, professors, and religious scholars debate and discuss and try to prove that God exists. The truth is evident and it's always there in front of us; it's just that we don't have the eyesight or we just don't concentrate on understanding it. Even if we understand, we are human—the most contentious in everything.

So my parents came to Navi-Mumbai and my father started a small business for the survival of his family. He did all that he could to make us happy and to give us a sustainable life where we could have a good education and a good life with all the basic needs and amenities. He felt it was his duty and responsibility, and he was committed to it with purity, and let me confess here, HE DID GOOD.

Then I came into existence in my mother's womb, and let me put more emphasis here on the word "creation," the creation which came into existence as all the billions before me and after came into this world.

Now here people never think about how this works. How does a life come into the wombs of women? Scientific evidence has given us knowledge about the embryonic development of a fetus and the development of a child in the mother's womb. Modern scientific inventions have helped us to know all about this and to understand the biggest creation of this world.

There are lots of people in this world who still don't know about the stages of embryonic development due to lack of education, lack of means, or lack of media.

I will focus on all these aspects of life in this book through a common man's point of view and capabilities; every single human can think and has that mental capability. One shouldn't have to be a scholar or scientist or philosopher.

I came into this world and was raised as all human beings are raised, with their parents' guidelines, their teachings and way of life, the same way their parents taught them, which may be a little better or more as there is always a betterment in life per the changing world and economy of the country where you live.

My parents taught me rituals and the teachings of the religion they had followed from their forefathers, and they taught me a belief in God and creation and human existence in this world as per their knowledge and the religious and school teachers.

Things were going along perfectly for my parents, but my mind was always asking questions. *What is going on in my life?* I used to question myself, and I saw nothing but a big QUESTION MARK.

Why am I learning these lessons?

Is this the lesson of life?

Is this the lesson of religion?

What is religion?

Do I have to follow it without question?

Do I have a choice?

Do I have to follow something else?

What do I want?

Where am I going?

Where is me in this?

What is my wish?

What are other things besides me?

All these questions made me slow in my studies and I always stayed behind in comparison to all those kids who were good, fast, and called to be scholars. And I found no answers to my questions from anyone.

The questions remained the same there till I grew up and I started thinking on my own and studying these questions with my own intellect. When I reached the age where I could use my own intellect and get all these answers to my questions, I was thinking in a different way. Let's see how I got the answer to all these questions and where I am today.

# Reality Begins

I WILL NOT say my story begins but rather reality begins with my coming into existence in the world. Every human being comes into the world the same way I did. And as I said in my introduction, we never give a thought about this big miracle and sign and signal which nature gives us about the creation of the human body.

In today's world everybody needs proof and miracles to prove the existence of a creator, which is again a big question and it's not been yet answered. Many believe there is a creator behind everything They give the creator names with their own words such as God, Allah, Bhagwan, etc.

I don't want to go into more detail about how to find where those words came from and look to history for their origin; this will be for those who have studied all of this. I am going to talk about the normal concept with normal language, using easy words and methodology with which we can come to a conclusion about questions like:

1) WHAT IS GOD?

2) DOES HE EXIST?

3) CAN WE GET PROOF OF GOD'S EXISTENCE?

4) WHY ARE WE HERE IN THIS WORLD?

5) WHAT IS THE PURPOSE OF OUR LIFE?

6) WHAT IS THE PURPOSE OF THE UNIVERSE?

I am sure there are millions of questions running through your mind right now:

What is this man talking about?

Does it make sense?

How he is going to conclude in the end?

Some people also have a habit of reading the end part of the book to see the conclusion, and they reach their own conclusions about books without read them in full. But they miss many points which the author wants to make in his books; the author wants to give a light of knowledge to this world, to the people, to help them get the truth in their own understanding, with their own capabilities, and talking in their own language.

Hence I will request the reader make notes while reading this book and compare your life with it and try to find the truth or conclusion which will give you immense harmony and peace—physically, mentally, and logically.

As I said, reality begins with our existence in this world; we come into life with a pure soul, knowing nothing about this world or relationships or traditions or religions or God or about our own life. No human is bad from childhood.

No one can deny they came with their own accord and having a knowledge of what they are going to be in the future—what they will do, what they will follow, in terms of everything. Hence we can say we came in this world as one nation, and that's the nation of humanity.

I don't want to quote from any scriptures nor am I quoting it. It's common sense which no one can deny that when we are born we are the same as a small child with no religion or worldly impurities or thoughts.

I am sure there are these kinds of statement in scriptures as we all know about it, but I would rather correlate these sentences with reality of human existence which starts from the mother's womb.

Every human being in this world comes with the same law and instruction and pattern which has been designed by nature for human birth on this earth, no matter which caste, creed, and religion it may belong to.

Humans have to come on this earth without knowledge of what they are.

What will they be in the future? A Muslim, a Hindu, a Christian, or a Jew?

What kind of religion are they going to follow?

These all come into the picture when people are born, and programming starts by their parents. No one can choose to be born in a Christian or Muslim or Hindu or Jewish or Buddhist family or any other religion of this world.

All human beings have one identification in common: we all are HUMAN BEINGS.

Being human, what have we achieved?

What have we done?

What are we going to do?

Nobody knows when they are just a small child. The soul does not yet have any impurities of world pictures or living styles, no classification when we are kids that this we belong to a certain religion, caste, creed, or name. We should be called CHILDREN OF HUMANS.

Here you will find the answers to your questions, which will ring a bell right there in your mind:

WHO AM I? WHY AM I WHAT I AM NOW?

The answer is in your mind already, which I think I don't have to mention, and it's you who has to think and decide WHO YOU ARE. WHO MADE YOU INTO WHAT YOU ARE TODAY?

Your parents gave you a name and identification to let you know that you are their son and they can call you that name so that others can know you with that name. And that name gives you their religion. You become what you are today without being asked for your option and without having any options.

You start growing up, developing, polishing yourself. How many of us here know about evolution theory? Not many? But let's not talk about this; we don't have to take any support of so-called theories which are beyond common man's reach or understanding. We will see all this with common examples and realities which are in front of our eyes. And we know it, we see it, but still we ignore it. We don't think about it. What is that? Our development is in the hands of our parents or guardians, which means evolution in our life.

We are taught right from the beginning how to walk, how to talk, and how to do everything that humans do in this life to live to be called good human beings in our society. It helps to make us different from the animals and to live our life sober. The organized way of life. Which makes us the most powerful living beings on this earth.

Then why do we need to be anything else other than a good human being?

It's something we didn't get from our own choice. We got it from tradition, we got it from our parents, they got it from their parents, and so on. We have no choice whether to accept it or not, but we have it pounded into ourselves unknowingly.

Why should we do the same things our parents are doing?

Why should they do the same thing their parents did?

Why are we doing all those religious practices and rituals? What we are following? Why can no one say that he did it with knowledge?

A doctor cannot be a doctor unless he gains the knowledge of his degree. Unless he studies. A professor can't get his degree unless he passes all his examinations from childhood till he is selected as a professor in the college or university.

Take any example of any individual and how they reached their achievement level and how they are known to all today with their so-called identification in this world.

Then why not in terms of their own religion?

A BIG QUESTION MARK AGAIN?

That's because there is no authority to check how right and how perfect you are in your belief. Or in your religion.

How perfect. Plus how have you passed your examination of so-called caste, creed, and religion you are entered into? You are promoted into it without your will or your choice. With no study, no knowledge, you have already passed your exam and you have succeeded to be called Muslims, Christians, Jews, or Hindus.

There are many questions like this. Think about it.

Anybody in this world can say:

I am a born doctor.

I am a born scientist.

Did any doctors ever say, "I am a doctor because I was born in a doctor's family"?

Did any scientist ever say, "I am a scientist because my parents were scientists"?

No...this sounds illogical. And stupid... People will laugh at this kind of person.

But now think about this:

When someone says I am Muslim or Christian or Jewish or Hindu, everybody will accept it. But at the same time if someone asks me how I became a Muslim, Hindu, or Christian, I plainly reply, "Because I was born in that family and my parents followed those religions, that's why." AH HA. That's not illogical now, and nobody cares, and that's acceptable without questions and certification or authentication or knowledge.

If someone asks me, "How did you become all this?" I have the plain answer about my parents and about my family belonging to that caste, creed, and religion.

If you ask someone what their parents did to become Christian or Muslim or Hindu, they will again reply that it's because they belong to that family. BIG LAUGH...

NOW, DOES THAT MAKE SENSE?

THINK ABOUT IT.

ASK YOURSELF THIS QUESTION.

As it is said, there is nothing in this world which is free. To get anything you have to pay for it. There is no achievement without process or without effort. In the same way, to become a real human or a real follower of any religion, what you are following or practicing now, ask yourself this question, which is, I think, enough to make you think about the reality of your own life, your own belief, or your own existence on this earth.

# Molding Begins

I USED THIS word "molding" specifically to signify how your life changes after you start developing your mind and your body with your surroundings and the people and the circumstances you are living within. Each event and uncertainty molds your life in different ways.

We become the same human being our surroundings want us to be, what our leaders want us to be, what our teachers want us to be, what our parents want us to be. A few things in us are different from others; they are in us, in our soul, a gift of nature. What cannot be changed are the traits of our personality.

Read carefully wherever I mention nature. Till now I have not mentioned anything that makes you think I am talking about God, that God made this and that. Then I would sound more like the translators of scriptures or a preacher in some church.

We start thinking...and thinking can be done in two ways: the way which has been shown to us and the way which we found by ourselves.

Here we think the same way our whole life, which is being taught to us by whom? By the people who influence us, by the preachers or teachers of our so-called religions, and the nearby events that make up our mind and teach us, give us direction to think in that way. We soon stop using our own mind and follow them, asking no questions and accepting that what they say is true as they are more knowledgeable than we are.

We start thinking, acting, talking, and behaving in the same way as others in our reach or doing what they want us to do. We have not been asked to choose one of the different types of religion, but we have been asked to follow without following what we are interested in and what we understand. We follow those in society. We keep on following unknowingly and we start practicing all that others do in our family.

We get teachings from elders in our family and from religious teachers how to perform rituals and we do so, not knowing if everything they say is true or false.

And in due course when we become adults, despite having the power of a thinking mind and intellectual potential, we don't have time to study these realities or myths, to verify how true or how false they are. What we follow in childhood we keep on following throughout our life. We are already programmed by religious personalities or teachers or preachers, thinking that it's beyond our power or capacity to think like them or talk like them or be a scholar like them.

LET ME ASK A FEW MORE QUESTIONS:

1) What makes that scholar a scholar in your eyes?
2) What makes him so popular that you accept whatever he says?
3) What makes him so pure that we feel he is God's loved one?
4) What makes him so prominent that we think we cannot be like him?

Again the answer is in your mind. And you know it well.

Then again my questions to all human beings:

1) Why can't we be like them?

2) What did they get from nature that we didn't?

3) What can they do that we cannot?

4) Are they not human like us?

5) Don't we all possess the same qualities and features?

The answer is in your mind and you know it. JUST THINK...

1) Then why is the molding of our life in their hands?

2) Why can't we make our own choices about practices and rituals?

3) Why can't we study the truth or the falsities about what we follow?

4) Why can we become humans and then have to become Christians, Jews, Muslims, and Hindus without having knowledge of our own religion?

After trying to search for truth, the right thing we find is what our way of life is, and that's the truth we have been seeking for decades. We will discuss this in detail and open more closed doors in your mind. You may think with your own mind, and you will get answers.

As of now, this chapter is not yet so clear. I am sure the answer lies within you. Do not let others mold your life without your permission because everything in this world can be stolen from you, but your mind and your heart are your own. You own them and no one else can steal them from you. Your intellect is your own, and no one else can hamper it. You should use it in the right way so that you can think wisely, discover the truth, find satisfaction, and get all the answers to your questions.

The common example involves the living things and the nonliving things on this earth which have some sort of influence molding them, their personality, their existence, and their shape.

We humans have superpower minds; we have the freedom to accept anything or reject anything. The same thing is applicable to your life, whether to accept what you are or what you want to be. But getting the truth by finding the truth and not from accepting what others says. And not what others follow.

Molding is on others till the age where you are not in a state of thinking or reasoning for the things happening in your life. In the adult stage you may go for truth or in search of Truth, through gaining knowledge of the things that raise questions in your mind.

All the natural phenomena and the collective information, which is easily accessible, may lead you toward truth, but you should reason. Ask yourself questions, and if you get the right answers, I am sure you will be satisfied with what you are following or doing.

We are not nonliving things that can be molded the way the pot of clay can be molded on the wheel; and we don't just remain passive, doing nothing, rather following others without questions and not trying to find peace of mind. We get relaxed, so we are happy, no need to think further. Remember, man learns from his mistakes and he keeps on learning till the end of his life.

In struggling to live this life and to earn a living, we forget to ask why we are on this earth.

Why are we on this earth?

How should we be on this earth?

The answer you will find within you.

# Development of Mind and Body

OUR MIND AND body play important roles in shaping our personality. The mind is the ultimate source of power and guidance, gifted by nature to all living beings. Human minds are more powerful than those of any other living creature in this world. We definitely don't need any proof to prove this.

Human minds are capable of storing and retrieving the information stored in it at lightning speed, and that's how what we do differs from other living beings, right from the beginning of our lives till the end.

The human mind is a great creation of nature and designed in such a complex way that we need no proof to prove it's a supreme creation and needs no comparison with any other creation on this earth.

The development of mind starts in our childhood till we become mature enough to understand, think, take action, and make conclusions on our own. The process takes time, and this process is called development or evolution. Everything, whether living or nonliving, takes time to come to its final stage or finished state, its complete, developed state.

There is beautiful word I found while studying different languages of the world. "Rubuyat" in Arabic means a process from its beginning stage till it's finished. That makes me think that every single nonliving and living being in this world goes through this process, so why not our belief or religion? I found the answer is that they do.

There is an important point in our belief and religion where these processes go through other's influence and injectors in our life and not with our own wish. Hence our mind does not think about it nor do we try to find out if what we are following is true or false. If taken with intellect, this process can go in a different way if we want.

Let's say when we are children our parents teach us about all religion, give us education about all the religions in this world, and give us a choice of what we want to follow. You can study and use your own intellect and choose to become a Christian, Muslim, Hindu, Jew, or any other. I don't think that has happened since human history developed.

No one ever thinks about it willingly or not. We have been forced emotionally, dramatically, and blindly to follow what has been followed by our forefathers. And we don't even know when we were brought into it. Some of us raise our interest and try to find out truth and study. I am sure we have the right path on which our creator has asked us to walk, and I am sure we have the real meaning of life and the real so-called God.

It's very important to understand these developments of our mind and our body and how we are using them in terms of anything and everything.

We see many preachers, debaters, religious leaders, and priests; we should listen to them but also study on our own what they are talking about. I have heard many of them talking about scriptures, and they say everything that has been written in scriptures without giving any reference of chapters or verses, and I ask them where it's written. I have been told many times, "Who cares where it's written? Who wants to know about that?" If people believe that it's in scriptures, let them believe it. Here I was amazed and I thought, *I don't want to follow what they themselves don't know they are advising*.

BIG QUESTION AGAIN: WHAT SHOULD WE FOLLOW?

The answer we have to find out ourselves in the same way we have to find our own way of life. I want to make clear that we don't need big philosophical minds; we don't have to be scholars to understand the scriptures. We can become more scholarly than so-called religious scholars if we study, if we get knowledge. The power of knowledge is the door of advancement, the right path, and the door toward truth.

We all should use our minds. Our intellect has been given in the same proportion to every human being, but it all depends on how we use it and how we develop it, through research, study, and investigation. Use your intellect with an open mind and heart and get the truth.

I would like to point out a very important factor in the advancement of every single human being, something that stops people from progressing their own knowledge in terms of religion: LANGUAGE.

We all grew up in different states, different communities, and different countries. We are different races, castes, creeds, and religion; we speak different languages. And our religious scriptures are in different languages; most of the time we don't understand. of the Quran, the Bible, Bhagavad Gita,

Yajurveda, and Chandogya Upanishad are in different languages like Arabic, Hebrew, and Sanskrit.

We may not understand it, but still we keep on reading the scriptures without understanding the language, as it's not our language. Those scriptures came with those messengers in those countries where the people speak those languages. The language barrier is the biggest barrier in human development in terms of the religion we are following.

We read it, recite it again and again, knowing not a single meaning from it, and we think we get virtues for that. Reciting something which is not understood...how can that give you virtue? Common sense. If someone speaks English and not French and I give him a French song to recite every single day so that he will get virtue from it, and the person does, what do you call him? An intelligent man? A man with a mind?

Why are scriptures like that? Why don't we take this seriously? When you are reading someone's translation, it is that person's understanding of the Arabic, English, Sanskrit, and Hebrew words. I am sure that will help you a bit to understand the meaning, but it is not 100 percent of your understanding. So you have to read translations, but you can also study the actual meaning by learning the pattern of the scripture and by searching the dictionary of that language, which will help you conclude whether what you are reading is right or wrong or whether it's properly translated.

We should understand first the language in which it's written. Now, I am not talking about mere language—there are different ways of representing sentences and expressing views. There are different ways to explain patterns, like

1) LITERAL SENTENCES

2) ALLEGORICAL SENTENCES

3) SYMBOLIC SENTENCES

4) NUMERICAL SENTENCES

Suppose someone says, "I SAW A SHIP OF THE DESERT IN THE SAHARA.

Now this statement can be understood in different ways by different people, as per their own understanding and interpretation. It is English but it still makes for different interpretations. Some might interpret it in a literal way, as in they saw some sort of vehicle which helps take them from one place to another in desert sand.

Some know how to read between the lines and the proverbs and riddles or derivation language; they know the perfect word for camel, which is also called a ship of the desert, and may interpret it the right way, that they saw a camel in the desert. Here that makes a huge difference in understanding the language; the statement which makes readers follow wrong things or right things.

I would suggest the translators crack the code behind the language rather than merely translating it word for word, and this should be explained in the beginning of the book—that some verses are literal and some of the verses are allegorical and so on.

BIG QUESTION AGAIN. Why do they do it? And why not?

The answer is in your mind; think and I am sure you will get your own answer.

Hence that's how the mind plays an important role in the development of our body—and our belief and our search for truth, what to follow and what not to.

Beliefs keep on changing as we keep on progressing in our study and knowledge. Beliefs cannot be a constant form of our state of mind.

# Thinking Power

AS WE TALK about mind and body and thinking, so many questions arise. The power of thinking is the strongest asset of our human body. Thinking power lets you determine the difference between truth and non-truth, between right or wrong, between yes or no.

In order to know the truth and what we are into, we have to be thinkers rather than just blind followers. We have to take knowledge from our own minds and we have to take knowledge from our surroundings and from every source which will take us to the right path.

We are so lost in imaginary worlds and materialistic worlds in our society and in our own lives that we don't think over the miracle which we see every single day in our own selves and in our surroundings.

When we think of what we own, we think of worldly and materialistic things like

How much money do we have?

What house should we buy?

What car are we going to buy?

Where will we travel?

Where to live? What to eat? What to wear?

All these normal necessitates of life are important, but besides that, what are we are missing is to think about every single thing we have, whether it is tangible, intangible, inside our body or near and around us in nature.

First we start with our surroundings: earth, space, trees, mountains, sky, water, birds, animals, fruits, and things like cars, household products, electronics. Anything and everything on this earth gives you some sort of sign and signal to understand where we got all these from. It was just like that—it happened and all the living creatures on this earth came into existence—size, shape, traits, and structure. All the metals products we got from the great discoveries of the scientists and doctors and astrologers—they are there from always since we tried to find them and tried to used them.

These are the biggest miracles that we can see in detail if we study with modern means of microscopes, telescopes, and scientific studies of this world, which has been created by some supreme power which we can call nature or creator or God.

There are detailed studies and debates going on every single day in each part of the world about the truth and what to follow and what not, and people need to know that miracle which proves that there is someone called God.

Our thinking power creates this question in our mind as we are in search of our own creator, as whoever it may be who created us has given us that power to think about him or our creator or nature or you can say God.

Nature has given us eyes to see, ears to hear, and intellect to think. That's why we are the most powerful creatures on earth. All these words, terms, and languages in which we are talking and reading and writing are our own creation. No one knows where it comes from; no one knows who created it; no one knows why it's been created in that way.

History shows the starting point, but how the words were collected and the alphabets arose in human minds, no one knows. Is it magic? This kind of question is always there without answer as it's too deep for human capabilities to know about it.

In the same way computers can't think the way they want, it's we humans who have given them memory, power, and processing speed, and we will keep on upgrading as we find new things. In the same way the one who created us has created us with some capabilities, he knows it but we know not.

We get stories of human creations in scripture and in books and in history that are to our own understanding; people wrote in books and we are reading them and trying to reveal the reality behind them. We have to think about our own body and how miraculous is it. Its work from our beginning till end is nonstop, and how complex is the creation inside our body which science has already proved. We can't deny its complex structure and architecture.

The biggest miracle, human beings and our thinking power, which we got along with the structural existence of our body, are an excellent combination that makes us powerful. So think on every single thing we see, hear, and do. These prove that there is someone with supreme power who has created the whole world and universe and galaxy and us, and that can be called God. The word for the creator can be uttered in different languages in different ways: God, Bhagwan, Lord, Allah, others.

So no matter what, we cannot deny that there is someone

who created all this. I am not concluding that there is a God; that we will decide once we reach our final chapter, **Existence of God.**

Here we are just thinking of the possibilities all around us and inside us, which makes us think about the miracles we see every single day.

Think for instance:

Why are we thinking about this question?

Is there is a god or not?

Why do we think that there is a god and we follow all these religions?

The answer is because we have freedom. We have freedom to think and to choose what we want and what we don't. It's up to us what we want to eat, drink, and perceive. The lion in the jungle cannot eat grass; it's been commanded by nature to survive on flesh and blood. A sheep cannot eat meat; it's beyond its nature to eat meat. But we have this freedom even after coming on this earth about what has to be done and what does not in every single thing.

We are capable enough to think about what is wrong and what is forbidden and what is not good for our health, but not a few things which are beyond our thinking capabilities and have been taught by our scriptures and followed for decades, like we cannot marry our sisters.

So man is gifted with the freedom to act as humans with enough potential to know what is right and what is wrong. We still make mischief and shed the blood of our own fellow beings.

How right is it? Think.

And for what it is? Again think.

Do we all, being one single type of creature, really differ from each other?

Does God really want us to follow all those religions? Races and tribes and castes?

Think...

If yes, why?

If not, then what?

So many questions, which we all have answers for in our own minds, but we don't want to accept it, we don't want to know it, we don't even bother about it.

Again there is a question to all:

What stops you from doing that?

What stops you from accepting that?

What makes you deaf, dumb, and blind?

What has happened to our minds?

What kind of blindness is this?

Why don't we use the strongest and the most powerful gift of nature in thinking about what we are up to?

And why do we think we are not one nation?

The creator has made us as an entire mankind. The word "mankind" is for all of us, no matter what caste, creed, and religion we belong to. The other living beings know us with this name, mankind, not with the name Muslim, Christian, Jew, or Hindu.

1) Why do we worship?

2) What do we worship?

3) What do we do if we don't?

4) What do we do if we do?

5) Does it really make a difference?

That's all we have to think and I am sure we will be on the right path in search of truth. We have to use our minds. Scientific study has proved with modern technology that an average man uses 25 percent of his mind throughout his life. Just imagine if we used 50 percent. Even 30 percent would make a difference.

There are signs and signals in nature for those who think!

# Search for Truth

NOW EVERYBODY IN this world is in search of truth.

Is there a god or not?

Which religion is true?

Which way do we have to follow?

Whatever we are following, how true and perfect is it?

And is our religion best?

Some may already have a mind-set that their religion is the best.

All these questions and concepts can be proven right or wrong on our own by going a little deeper into it, easily and slowly.

How does that work? And how will we know if whatever we are looking for is right and that we are not on the wrong path of life?

In search of the truth, some of us approach religious leaders, priests, or scholars and seek information about the real truth. We get some information from them and we take it for granted that their explanations are perfect and truthful, and we follow the same.

BUT WHERE ARE YOU IN THAT?

We don't know that the information is perfect and pure or right. That's the other person's perception, and if you follow that, it means you are following that person because he explained it to you, and you accepted it without doing your own study.

In terms of world study, we have teachers, and teachers teach us how to learn, but along with that we do our own study too; mere teaching from teachers is not enough. When we do our own study from the sources we have, we pass our examinations with good scores. We read and write until we graduate. But in religious terms, the teacher is the creator and his message is around us, inside us, in the scriptures, and maybe in our existence.

We have to find it on our own, and I am sure we will get our degree from the creator itself. Don't think that what scholars can do we can't do; we need to start from somewhere.

No matter how late it is, no matter how slow it is, no matter how imperfect it is, everything has its start. It will soon be starting inside you, and you will see this world with open eyes, an open heart, and an open mind. With no covers on your eyes, with no deafness in your ears, and with no bondage on your mind.

The search for truth leads you to the right path; the right path leads to the right destination; the right destination leads you to the truth, and then you can decide on your own what God is, what religion you should follow, or even whether to follow any religion at all. Or is a simple belief in a creator enough?

Research takes you to the place which is already there and you discover it; research finds new inventions; research takes you to those miracles which are hidden in nature, and you can reveal them. There is so much in this earth and the universe which is still to be discovered—all the creation of the mighty power whom you may call God, Supreme Power, or Nature.

These are mere words. The acceptance of nature and its creation makes you accepting that there is something more powerful, and the most eternal and most unknown to our naked eyes. Voluntarily or involuntarily, nobody can deny this fact, that all these creations on the earth and in the universe itself are from a creator. It can be a phenomenon to us or it can be a miracle to us.

In search of truth, people arrange seminars, meetings, discussions, debates, and try to find the truth behind the creation of human beings and this universe. And the discussion is still going on.

The answer is still hidden. Why? I am trying to explain this with a little example, let's say a man-made creation. We have the power of thinking and capabilities to invent and to create a few things on this earth. I will use the example of a computer here; that sounds to me more similar to the creation of nature in several aspects.

A computer has:

1) Memory
2) Processing power
3) Task-making ability
4) Ability to help people
5) Its own shape and size
6) Life and durability

7) A fuel source (electricity)

8) Different capacities, sizes, shapes, and color.

We humans created it. We gave the computer all of its specifications, which we designed. Let's say a computer is able to do anything on its own, which allows it to judge human capabilities. Sounds a little illogical, but it may help you think about what you think about your creator. A computer cannot go beyond its boundaries which have been assigned to it by humans.

In the same way, no matter how much you search for the final conclusion—is there is a god or not and what are his capabilities—we don't have those beyond-boundary-level capabilities in us because only he who created us, the creator, knows what capabilities he has given us. We can get his signs and signals in this existence that may make us think about his presence and about his capabilities, which are immense and unimaginable and immeasurable in terms of his creations of this whole universe and its arrangement and its continued balance, sustaining in each and every single microsecond of this life on the earth and universe.

The latest research in geography, science, anatomy, biology, chemistry, and astronomy give a big signal and marks of miracles that a little imbalance in nature's law and its system and its arrangement tends to collapse the whole foundation and coexistence of the universe and living life.

In search of truth people read books, browse the Internet, talk to people, watch documentaries, and try to understand the myth behind human existence, which is actually inside you, around you, visible to your eyes every single second, heard through your ears, uttered with your sound, and felt by your soul. But mostly we don't think.

When a small child raises his or her voice when something goes wrong, what's that? Have you ever thought it's by default that man has the power and instinct to identify what is wrong and what is right? Then why when we grow up, we don't use this power, as we don't think—we react, we act, without thinking.

Try to understand, analyze, and then take needed measure; that's the best way of resolving our problems and taking charge of our actions to the betterment of life. But that action can be as fast as lightning, for which we need that practice and that habit which we left far behind when we were growing up.

Truth is always there; we have to search for it in the way we are capable. Every person has their own way of understanding and identifying things and situations. Some may take time, some may not—it's all on us how we are taking into consideration those issues and problems which come in front of us and how we solve them. If we do it in the right way, we will get the right results, and if not the consequences have to be borne by an individual.

If there is mystery, there is always a way to solve it; we just have to find it and think carefully on each and every aspect in connection to it. The people in this world try to search things, do their own study, and conclude their own conclusions; that's their own individual understanding. Don't follow it. Listen to it, learn from it, and try to do your own study. That will surely take you to the desired destination of the truth you are looking for.

# Life Struggle

THE WORD "STRUGGLE" can be taken into consideration in different ways. Let's take it in terms of all living beings in connection to us. Every human being on this earth, right from its birth till death, struggles to live and also to earn a livelihood and take care of the basic needs of life. While doing this we forget about all the good things and bad things going on around us and inside us. The question mark lies in our heart always, and we think we know the truth.

We follow what has been followed by others and billions around us without knowing the facts, what is right or wrong, or what sort of corruption has been cooked with the reality we know and we are into.

Many people think that some of their country's laws are good for them and some of them are not. The act of denying things is always there in us; some do it with knowledge and some without knowledge. The effects are bad and sometimes good.

We run behind everything we want, and few of us run behind truth. Try and read those scriptures that have been sent unto you by the creator, and see how true those are. See how perfectly they are arranged, and try and understand their language—not in a literal sense but in all the senses. They are trying to teach you something which has no contradiction, and the concept should be universal in that no one in this world can deny it.

Many people think that the right path or the truth or guidance will come to them eternally without seeking it, studying it, or trying to find it from the creator by default, which is a wrong concept. In this world nothing comes of its own; there is always a source, an origin we have to find. We have to look for it, and we have to discover it.

There are sources for it, there are ways for it, and there are methods for it which have to be followed in the sequence or format or type they are supposed to be. The mysteries are yet to be solved, and the truth is yet to be discovered, which is there hidden from your eyes, hidden from your ears, and hidden from your mind. Try to explore it and you will see miracles you never, ever imagined.

There are people who are in their old age now, and when the light of knowledge comes to them, it's hard to accept for some, and some embrace it with open arms. Some feel that what they have been doing throughout their life is in vain if they accept the new discoveries, so they prefer to stick to their old concept, and they want people around them to do the same. If not they react in different ways: aggression, calmness, quietness, rejection, anger, and in some cases protest.

But again the truth lies beneath, and sometimes it gets dumped, sometimes it gets ignored, and sometimes it gets erased by powerful influences. But still truth is truth; no one can erase or delete it for good.

Every single human being is struggling in this world in one way or another to sustain their life in a perfect or at least a good way. Now voluntarily or involuntarily, they abide by the law of sustenance. No matter what caste, creed, and religion they are from, they abide by the law of sustenance, which is made by the creator. Now you may call it God, Allah, or Bhagwan.

This law of sustenance is universally applicable for each and every living and nonliving, tangible and intangible thing on this earth. We all rise up from childhood to adolescence, from adolescence to adult, and from adult to old, and we pass on like that.

Everything in this universe has starting and end points. So no matter where we are, no matter who we are, we abide by this law to live our life. All living beings need food and all living beings have a way of life.

We have choice, freedom, and intelligence. We are free to choose how to live our life, we are free to choose our actions, we are free to think about what we will be in the future, and we are free to do everything on this earth on our own, with our own, and in our surroundings and other creations in connection to us.

We have to think about the creator and its law, not about the creations and their laws. We are in the world, which has cities and towns and villages, and every country, city, or town has its laws. Then what about this human body? On whose law is it running? On whose system is it working? What if we do not follow these laws? What would be the result? Many big questions again. I am sure many of us haven't thought about this ever.

We struggle to earn a livelihood, and we try to live a good life, but there are many who haven't seen this good life right from childhood. The law of sustenance is the same for all. It changes for no one, and whether you want to or not, you have to follow it without question. But you get something extra which other living creatures don't have, and that's freedom of choice, freedom of thinking, and freedom of using your own mind.

For example: Animals cannot choose their own food; they abide by the law of nature which has been assigned to them. The lion cannot eat grass; it's been assigned to eat meat or flesh. But the goat, on the other hand, cannot eat meat and she has to eat grass. That's the law of nature, in the same way the day is followed by night, the moon followed by the sun, and the universe is followed by the galaxy—it's all in this law. Willingly or unwillingly, they have no choice but to follow their duties and responsibilities with commitment and purity.

Then why can't we human beings? Again a question mark. Why do millions of us live below the poverty line, and why are there corruptions and consequences which make human life miserable and hard? I don't want to go into politics now, but the reason behind all this is that we have no knowledge of what we are doing without thinking, and we think sometimes for ourselves in the wrong way, not knowing what the consequences for others will be. But anyway, nature's law is always there, and the effects and consequences are borne by us only.

I am sure if each and every person started thinking about the effects of his deeds and what he is doing in advance, this earth would be like heaven, which is still a myth. I don't think there is a hell or a heaven seen by any one of us; no one has come back after death to show us or to tell us about it. It's a rather allegorical form of statement that explains our life from the lower stage to the higher stage, which can be compared to the life in hell or in heaven.

Take for example a man who is homeless and begging for money for food because of his bad deeds or bad habits, and all of a sudden someone sees a strength in his personality that can be used for something in this world and which can be paid for in terms of job. If he accepts it and earns a good living, for him the life when he was homeless is hell, and the life after that with his own apartment and all the amenities, with job in hand, is heaven.

So everything is in this earth that we need eyes to see, and instead of struggling to live our life, we should plan to live it in the right way, with commitment and purity. No matter what job we are doing, no matter our position, we are not homeless, and we are not lacking in three basic needs: food, clothing, and shelter.

In all this we forget the law and the responsibility we are to abide by in default. We have no choice but to accept it as we are already on this earth, whose system is being run by its creator and whose laws are unchangeable for anyone. A little change in that law is the end of everything.

We forget this truth and this search is there in us and around us—what's in the present, what's in the past, and what's in the future is all there. We should have eyes to see it, we should have ears to hear it, and we should have intellect to use and to solve all these mysteries. I am sure no matter how many years have passed or how many years it's been said in scriptures, we will find more mysteries, as they are there from always. We need to shape them and use them in the right way to make our life like heaven on earth.

Life's uncertainties are the consequences of something; there is always a reason for what is happening with us and around us and in nature. We have to find how it happened and why and how we can correct it. And there's always a solution for it.

Life's struggle will not be that difficult if we all think about these things with an individual responsibility and the authorities on their level and the leaders in their level, but the solution must be applied with commitment and purity. I would like to use as our slogan here: "UPHOLD YOUR COMMITMENT AND BE PURE."

Now, thinking about all this will also lead by default to the ultimate question of whether there is something called God or not. I am sure you have a little knowledge, and if it's not yet clear, I will shed more light in the next topics.

# Purpose of Our Life and Survival

IT'S A BIG question again. What's the purpose of our life? It's been discussed and debated many times in various scriptures, seminars, events, lectures, and functions where people talk about religion and God and the existence of God. Now let us try and think with our own logic and general knowledge and not put pressure on the mind to study thousands of books and scriptures.

Why we are here on this earth? Where does this question arise from? Why does it arise? And what's the answer?

First, we have come to such a level of development of our body and mind that a complex question like "Why are we here on this earth" is raised in our own mind. That shows how important we are and why we are here. As I said earlier, there is always a reason behind everything. We have come so near to the creator's creation that we are wondering why he created all this, including us. The answer is there in our own minds.

Secondly, we have seen so many creations of nature around us, living or nonliving, tangible and intangible—what are those there for? We know some of the reasons for them, and they might not know that we are using them. They come to life and they have their own end. For example, a chicken comes to life and then it's our food, with different flavors and recipes. The chicken might not know why she came into this world along with all other creations and living beings, but she serves the purpose of being food for humans; likewise, animals to animals, plants to plants, plants to animals, etc. In the same way, there might be some other purpose related to humans' creation, and for that we have not been given the capability or understanding that can been seen with our eyes or that can been seen with our own existence, but surely there is a reason behind it that the creator knows.

Thirdly, we can look at this concept more closely and go a little deeper to learn the reason and how is that? Look at us. Each individual is a single person with our own identity, name, address, phone number, etc., but have you ever thought about how we have a qualities of somany people in one body. how so many people diffrent traits inside one body , and these traits make you diffrent person at different situation and that gives you diffrent identification in the eyes and minds of different people watching you . these comes in effect as per the want of circumstances time, event, surroundings, situation do you ever thought about this we play multiple personality role in our daily life. ? No, I am sure not many of us had ever thought about this.

Examples of personality traits:

1) Angry
2) Calm
3) Helpful
4) Aggressive
5) Challenging
6) Destructive

7) Innovative

8 Enthusiastic

9) Competitive

10) Multitasking

There are lot of traits in one individual that differ from person to person; these traits give you a specific identity, sometimes for good or on a permanent basis and sometimes for the time being.

Let's say a person in need seeks help from another person, and the other person helps him. For the person in need, the other person is like an angel, but if the other person scolds him and shouts and uses abusive words for his asking for help, that other person is a devil for him. Both angels and devils are there in us, so how can we say for what reason and purpose are we here in this earth? The answer can be too big or wide or it can be too complex to answer, but we can see more closely that we might be here for our spouses; we might be here for our parents, who are already here; we might be here for our children, who might be coming in the future; we might be here for all the inventions we've created so far.

If we take it individually, I am sure the answer to why we are here lies beneath. No matter why we are here, we have to perform our duties and responsibilities that have been assigned to us with commitment and purity and in the right way. We have to learn the ways of those who were successful before us; we have to learn good things and ignore bad things. Angels and devils are both in us, so there is a possibility of making mistakes and doing bad deeds, but we should think how to make it correct and avoid it. I am sure the results will be great.

We are knowingly or unknowingly following the creator's law and nature's law without asking any questions. No matter who the human being is, how big or small or what race, we all have to follow the same start and end of life with all that has been fixed and certain in this world. He the lord of the universe, the creator of all, no matter what word is used. There is something supreme which is beyond our imagination level and capability, but it's there always, everywhere in everything, in our immune system, which is working twenty-four/seven from our birth to our death.

It's there in our body, mind, and soul, and it's there in us everywhere, the law, the system, the method, and the commitment made by each and every living and nonliving things is being done with no questions to change it or not to do it. We go by a set of instructions to be followed without changing its code or system in order to change the life as per our desire. If we try to do that, that's the end of that life or thing.

So the answer to the above BIG question is in front of you, and I don't think we need any more explanation other than this: We think and we find the answer within ourselves.

So the purpose of life is to be known to the creator, and we can see signs and signals of it around us; that's is enough for us to understand that yes, there is reason behind every creation, in connection to others at least.

# Teachings and Rituals

NOW HERE IS an important aspect of our life that we are given without choice from birth. It's being taken into consideration, with no choice, that every single birth on this earth comes by the will to be Christian, Hindu, Muslim, Jew, and so on.

Being born in that family gives an ultimate identification for the newborn baby right from his childhood, and by keeping his name, he becomes the so-called religion's follower, which he doesn't even know about and which is not his own choice. Here's the important role religious teachers like our parents play, along with relatives and religious scholars who give us an idea and picture of that religion in which we were born. There is no comparison and no choice as to which one is better or which one is wrong and which one is right. The individual isn't allowed to decide which one to follow using his own intellect, doing his own study, research, and investigation in the light of knowledge and reality and history, studying everything on this earth which has been made by humans and followed by us. We humans have no authentication proving which one is right and which one is wrong. I am sure there is nothing wrong in any religion except its own exploration, which we never did.

So the followers are following their forefathers and they will ask their children to follow the same, and this will keep on going. It's our mind-set and it's a programming by all those forefathers and all those among us who are following these rituals and teachings which we feel are a must in our lives and give us a life after death. No one knows what happens after death; no one has come back to tell us.

These teachings and rituals of so-called religions have been followed by people without knowledge of where they come from. How authentic are they? And does God want these rituals? We still do them and we make ourselves happy by performing those rituals and we think we are pleasing God. That's what millions of followers do.

Rituals play an important role in impressing God, making him happy, and remembering God and his teachings, but we don't try to find out where these rituals came from. How authentic are the scriptures that teach those rituals? Big questions again. I am sure if we try and pound ourselves a bit in the scriptures, we will find the truth.

Few among us deny those scriptures, and there are a few questions for those people also. How can we come to know then about the laws and system about, for example, not marrying one's sister or brother? How do we know that we can't marry our fathers? This important and crucial information came from somewhere. There are those many questions marks again, and the answers are out there. In order to learn how true something is and how false or how important it is, we have to study, investigate, and gain knowledge of it. The biggest question is:

DOES GOD NEED THESE RITUALS?

Now this is bit complex and complicated. We will find our answers, as I said, if we pound ourselves in our scriptures. Rituals make us think that they are important for praising God. Millions of us think in this way. How authentic are they?

We have to find out, and I am sure we all can use our own intellect and gather information about this. Once again, let me remind all my readers, do not pound yourself in someone else's understanding; that's his understanding. Read, think, and make your own decisions, try to find the most authentic source or guide for all these questions, the ultimate guide. If it is there on earth, I am sure it's going to be in front of your eyes and you will find all the answers for the questions of what you are doing and what you are not supposed to do.

Creator, God, supreme power—whatsoever you call upon, if it's that mighty, does it need those rituals to be praised or to be remembered? THINK.

What are the roots of the existence of these rituals? What do they signify? What if we don't do them?

Again thousands of questions, and these questions will ring a bell in your mind about the right path and the truth. Millions of us follow these rituals and teachings without question or without studying their roots and without knowledge of how they came into existence and without understanding the method and logic behind them. We just follow these rituals and teachings like those who mock and copy.

Does the creator show the methods to do these rituals? If yes, where? In a book? Who wrote it? How authentic it is? You need to know everything, as no work without knowledge is perfect; it's called blind work with half knowledge, and half knowledge is dangerous.

I don't want to give you any references here for any books; you are intelligent enough to find this out. And I am sure you can do it. So let's try and find the knowledge. Why not?

# Religious Study

WHEN IT COMES to religious study or religious topics, people think that we have to leave everything behind and be away from this world to get the knowledge of the religion or the creator. This is just a mind-set or a program that has been installed in our mind. We have to get out of it first and foremost, and I am sure we can study religion or the creations and the creator while performing our normal life activities. We just need a little concentration and to use our minds to think over the situations happening near us, around us, and with us—in nature, in the world, and in the universe.

Religious study helps us to gain more knowledge and then we can decide on our own what the difference is between truth and myth. We have to understand the difference between the words "Lord" and "God." A god is a supreme power, a creator. But the Lord? Can it be God? Or any high-ranking authority who tries to teach us or give us the knowledge of our creator?

Think about it. Again, a BIG question.

I am sure you will easily be able to find the answers without going deep into thousands of books or scriptures. In today's world of modern means and technology, it's not that hard to get information about something like this. A little effort in our own mind will make everything clear about these kinds of questions.

No study in this world can be done by force! Even a small kid in school—if he is not interested on his own about some subject or topic and if we force him, we turn the student into a dull kid. His interest takes the student to a brighter level. Study cannot be done by force, so studying religion by force makes us more deaf and dumb, and we find ourselves nowhere, instead being the puppet of religious scholars and our teachers with no knowledge of where our own mind or our own intellect is going.

Any study should be by choice, not by force, as even the creator has given us that freedom to live our life on our own will and style and choice. So how can one be so mentally bonded with this kind of teaching? We should come out from this BOX and think beyond such boundaries with an open heart, mind, and eyes.

It's a normal human tendency: When we want to buy something, we have a choice and we think, with our own research, our own likes and dislikes, and we shop around and see what is the best suited to all our wants and budget and capabilities, and we buy those things. Why isn't it like that in religious study? Why do we take for granted that we are born in a particular family or community and we follow the same religion without any question or without asking to choose?

The question is logical. There are those who think that kids are not able to choose, so that's why they have to teach them all of this from their childhood. Let me tell you, they are doing nothing but programming their minds, the same thing they have gone through with their parents and so forth. Let them come to the stage where they will be capable; until then we can teach them about normal, good things and bad things in life so they can use their own minds and intellects and power to understand all about religion, God, and the creator. You can also teach them about the religion you are following, but along with that you should teach them what the other religions of this world say. And you should also ask them to decide what to follow when they are old enough to know the difference between right and wrong. This way they will not have the wrong mind-set about others in this world. We are all one nation of mankind, no matter what color, race, and community; we all came from the same ancestors.

This will make your kids brighter, with open minds and eyes to accept and follow the religion which is right, and they will be capable of knowing the difference between truth and myth. This is the right of every human being who has been left faaaaaar behind.

Why are these studies being done with no choice? In schools and colleges and universities, there are different publications to choose from in order to pursue our degree or diploma in education. Why are there different choices of fields? The son of a doctor can be a born doctor, why not the son of the astronaut can be a born astronaut. As in that case, we have to study and get our degree or certification.

Here is another big question: Again, why not in religion?

Where does this religion come from and why is it so important to follow?

Even if it is right to follow, everyone should have the right to think and to get the right knowledge. And I am sure if we all think about this and try to get knowledge of this, we can make one nation on this earth, and that's the nation of MANKIND—with heaven-like life, with freedom for all and peace for all, no fights for land, no fights for power, no fights for religion.

THINK ABOUT IT.

# Existence of God

BIGGEST QUESTION, BIGGEST MYTH, BIGGEST DEBATE, BIGGEST DISCUSSION, BIGGEST TOPIC.

DOES GOD EXIST? All those things we worship on this earth, are those really God? What is the difference between LORD and GOD? We have been talking about these words in this book right from the beginning, and we have come across some understanding. I am sure with this last topic, more myths are going to be clarified and will be opened in front of you to make you understand the truth of the biggest question: Does God exist?

This search for God has been going on for millennia, since the first step of humans on this earth. If you study history you will come to know that man was always curious about his own creator. And for millions of years humans have tried to find out whether there is a God. What does he look like? Where does he sit? And where is his kingdom or the place where he watches and creates all living beings and things on this earth and in the universe?

The imagination power and thinking process and lack of ways and means of investigation and development of human life toward the advancement of the secrets of God's creations make us think about his existence as per the capacity and the means available at that time in the pre-religion era to think of the most powerful visible power on the earth as God. Man learned the words and the language came into existence and they tried to express the creator in words like God, Allah, Bhagwan, and so on. Among them there were a few intelligent people trying to work in this direction who were trying to find out who had created the world, them, and the universe.

A few of them looked into nature, a few of them in their house, a few of them in themselves, and they tried to discover the existence of God therein. They came up with their own imaginings to glorify the creator's creation, and being impressed with it they thought to make its existence visible to make people aware of the creator's existence. Some went in the right direction and some went in the wrong and tried to make idols of the god. Some of them thought the sun was a god; some of them thought the moon was a god, some of them plants, some of them man himself, and some of them thought everything that showed the immense power of the creator and gave them benefit was a god.

This magical thinking started working in the minds of the humans, who started thinking and trying to find things which already existed but were yet not discovered. They tried to find those things hidden and discover them for their own use. This thing spread so fast in human civilization that every one of every tribe, sect, and place on the earth thought that all should praise the creator; this was something so immense that we humans could not imagine doing so and we could not create these kinds of creations. All the findings and discoveries seemed to be too small to the humans in front of the universe and creations in it, and we have such strong minds and thinking power that man came to know that there is something more powerful than himself. And that is the creator.

Man tried to praise these creations by praising the creator, and he tried to find his own way to praise the creator, and hence the visible gods and rituals came into existence. We are still talking about the era where there was no religion yet. The concept of God traveled all around the globe in each part of the world where humans existed. Every tribe derived the new ways and means to visualize the creator and to praise it, and they started giving it names and making methods of praising it as per their satisfaction and level of understanding.

After a few years, this led to various tribes creating various religions with different names and gods with visual representation. Man understood that there was a creator who made all these creations, including mankind, and then he tried to understand the reason for his own existence, which led him toward more discoveries about God and his existence. Henceforth, the concept was so popular that everybody accepted it—that there is a creator for everything and everybody in this earth and universe. Praising the creator was the humans' idea; there is no authentic proof that God or the creator himself came to earth and told us to praise him for creating them. This was a human idea. And yes, it was very valuable for everybody to know about such a complex creation of everything.

The concept kept on developing, with thousands of God images and thousands of rituals and practices to praise God. A few of them were cruel, a few of them were good, a few of them had no meaning, and a few of them made no sense, and that's because of man's mind and thinking power which can create these things on earth. On the other hand, yes, for sure there was a creator of everything, and that creator wanted to make a difference between the animals and humans. The creator has the power to create us and has power over everything.

This was getting immense in a crazy way, and man started using his mind beyond the imagination level, not knowing what was right and wrong. He started to act like an animal, abusing the life which had been given by the creator. The creator decided to teach the right way of life to the people, to make them stand apart from the other living beings as more powerful and more intellectual. He started guiding one among us and sent his message through him to the different parts of the earth. We call them saints, messengers, or prophets.

But those people were taken in the wrong way. Some people liked the concept of a right way of life. Some didn't and would not follow it, and some made those messengers into gods. Again here it shows that God has given us freedom to accept or not to accept, as we have intellect which makes us think and gives us the power to differentiate between right and wrong.

Hence the teachings and messages were given from the creator to us, to live our life and to progress and to bring system, law, and order to the human race, to separate us from animals. No one can say they have seen God. This is our imagination. Some of us remember God in terms of idols or images, and some of us think there is no image. What is right and what is wrong? I am saying here that we are able to think about it.

The tribes went on increasing the god images and the idols kept changing, but the concept was one—that there was a creator and we could say it however we wanted in whatever language, and we called him God. This is a concept in our mind and its human creation. Scientific studies and theory can only give us an idea or knowledge about the extent of the creator, but we have no such power to find out where the creator is hiding. He has given us a certain level of power beyond which we cannot think, but that power is far superior than that of any other living being on this earth.

Hence, to follow the religion or to follow rituals, that's our choice. It's not necessary to praise God. God has already created us. He doesn't need our praise for it. It's our choice; if we want we can, but then again why is it important? More big questions. Does it make any difference in our life? Does it have anything to do with our progress?

Can we not live our life with laws and systems, with no bloodshed, no difference between human beings, and we all live as one nation? Nation of mankind with creators way of life and the way we have in our developed world without making any fights on religions and sects which are humans creations?

# Conclusion

So, does God exist?

This question has come from us. We have created it and we created the concept of God, and we have to decide whether there is a god or not rather than discussing it on national or international levels. No one can force another to accept a religion. We are all born free, with intellect to live this life in PEACE like heaven, which no one can deny.

We created the concept of God and we believe that there is definitely someone behind the creation of the world and the universe, and that creator is God as God or Allah, Bhagwan, and so on. Just imagine if we all spoke one language and believed in the creator. Would we need different methods of praising him? If yes, why? If not, why not?

The answers are there within yourself and you will get it. Just try to become good humans and you will get everything you want in this earth. Uphold your commitment and be pure; that's the only thing the creator wants from you. That's what we are all missing.

Thanks to all my readers. I request that you think before pursuing anything without knowledge, and I am sure the truth will be in front of you.

Thanks.
Regards,
Uzair M. Ghole
uzairghole@ovi.com

CPSIA information can be obtained
at www.ICGtesting.com
Printed in the USA
LVOW13s1750300917
550696LV00015B/2122/P